Balmoral

Every man and his dog

Robert and Sarah Billington

Sunday afternoon sailing

Edward and island

Preface

Balmoral Beach represents all that is wonderful about living in and visiting Sydney. Long, lazy summer days enjoyed by picnickers on the lawn, fishermen on the jetty, nappy-clad toddlers taking their first tentative steps along the promenade, swimmers lapping up the sun and the water, rollerbladers darting, lovers strolling, and bridal parties posing... an atmosphere of celebration is pervasive.

Yet Balmoral is also a chameleon. On week days, its loud, crowded and glamorous side gives way to a stillness that is only disrupted by a barking dog, an occasional seagull screaming for someone's chips, or the soothing sound of the sea pulling gently in and off the beach.

The evenings bring the sophistication of restaurant crowds, anchored yachts and a promenade whose lamps highlight the elegance of its Port Jackson fig trees and Balmoral's best known landmark, the Rotunda.

On a sunny day Balmoral seems expansive. On a stormy day Balmoral is no less beautiful but seems to contract and brood. Even the Island can change – from a child's adventure land or a romantic hiding place for teenage lovers to a dark and mysterious Gothic outpost, filled with sinister secrets.

There are many interesting and beautiful beaches in Sydney, but none can claim Balmoral's rich history: its Aboriginal culture, the artist and gypsy encampments, dance halls, Theosophist-funded amphitheatres, statues commemorating dogs (and signs warning against them), as well as a coastline that features two pretty beaches perfectly divided by a small peninsular.

All the photographs were taken by Robert Billington between 1994 and 1996.

Sarah Billington

June 1997

The rockpools

OPPOSITE: *The Bathers' Pavilion*

Chief Boongarie

Don McLaren described King Boongarie as "...perhaps, Mosman's first 'con man'..."

The Sydney Gazette, November 27, 1830 recorded his death on Garden Island and referred to him as, "His Aboriginal Majesty, King Boongarie". Known as the "Supreme Chief" of the "Sydney Tribe", Boongarie hunted and fished on the northern shores of Port Jackson for many years and one of his "royal residences" was a Balmoral Beach cave.

Boongarie was born around 1770. He became known after Matthew Flinders chose him to be an interpreter on a voyage of exploration between Moreton Bay and Hervey Bay, on the "Norfolk" in 1799. Boongarie was described by Flinders as "...the worthy and brave fellow whose good disposition and manly conduct had attracted my esteem." In 1802 and 1803 Boongarie again joined Flinders, on the "Investigator", in a quest to chart the Australian coast. Boongarie became the first Aborigine to have sailed around Australia. His shipmates had a half moon brass plate made up which proclaimed his title as "King Boongarie, Supreme Chief of the Sydney Tribe".

Boongarie became famous in Sydney. His wife was referred to as "Queen Gooseberry". However, he also appeared to have other wives, known by such names as Askabout, Boatman, Pincher, Onion and Broomstick.

ABOVE: Sailing, Hunter's Beach.

OPPOSITE: Aboriginal cave off the Esplanade.

In 1815 Governor Macquarie assisted Boongarie, along with his family and another sixteen Aboriginal families, to settle at what is now known as Georges Heights. Macquarie provided them with boats, fishing nets and wheat seeds. Boongarie, who was credited as a talented diplomat, evidently took note of the fact that Governor Macquarie was the first military Governor of the Colony. He responded by ceasing to wear his naval uniform and instead adopted the uniform of a full colonel.

During World War II the Royal Australian Navy named the HMAS Bungarie in his memory.

Paraphrased from *Tales of Old Mosman*

Sunbather, Edward's Beach

"In the early nineties, one of the few cottages which existed in the area was used as a rest home for nurses. The story goes that: the old matron in charge complained to police that boat crews were in the habit of bathing off the beach in the nude. Sergeant Bultitude was sent by the Water Police to make enquiries. When he pointed out that the nurses' cottage was at such a distance from the beach that no one could possibly determine whether the offenders were dressed or otherwise, the matron replied: "We are positive. We distinctly saw them through field glasses."

Sydney Sails

Surf life savers practising off Balmoral

OPPOSITE: *Swimmer, yacht and rocks*

Y esterday the A.S.N. Company's steamer "Illalong" was chartered by Messrs. Taylor and Drysdale for the conveyance of New Year's Day excursionists to the Balmoral Gardens at Hunter's Bay in the Middle Harbour. The steamer took passengers down at half-past 10 am, at half-past 12, and 3, and brought the wearied holiday folks back to Sydney all the better for their breezy trip. The large airy shed adjacent to Mr Edwards' cottage was thronged with dancers throughout the day, encouraged by the exhilarating strains of Herr Apples' excellent brass band. Others, of the sterner sex, we saw perspiring freely in the open grass plot, under the excitement of the cricket ball; and others, male and female, were strolling about, botanising and conchologising, and colloquizing together."

Historical Anecdotes and Miscellany, 1930

Sunday afternoon cricket

Wanted, a Wharf at Balmoral

There is a difference of opinion existing at present as to whether there should or should not be a wharf at Balmoral Beach.

Those who oppose the project say that it would bring an objectionable class of people into Mosman. That seems to be their principal contention.

Those in favour of having a wharf urge that it would be a means of increased funds to the borough, which could be used in various ways to the benefit of the ratepayers; and that there is no reason to suppose objectionable people would intrude themselves upon our higher altitudes. In fact, whereas at present everyone who wishes to go to Balmoral must come through Mosman, if there were a wharf, and a regular service to the beach, they could get there without coming so near our most cherished aloofness.

We are told that there are several companies who have already offered to relieve the Council of all risk by building suitable wharfage accommodation, on which they would pay an equitable royalty to the borough.

There can be no doubt that it is only a question of time. The tendency of things in Mosman is towards wider interpretation of the "Open Door" policy. All classes must be considered equally; the good of all must be looked to. Mosman does not belong to a few selfish people, but to all decent citizens.

The wharf would give increased facilities for health and enjoyment to thousands in less salubrious suburbs; it would therefore be good for them. It would bring increased revenue to the borough; it would therefore be good for the ratepayers. The Council would be in a better position for effecting improvements in streets, which would be good for all residents.

It seems, from a thoughtful consideration of the question, that a wharf would be directly or indirectly beneficial to everybody. By all means, then, let us have it, and as soon as convenient.

The *Mosman Mail,* 1 September 1899

OPPOSITE: The Manly Ferry ploughs across the Heads.

ABOVE AND OPPOSITE: Bathers in the mist

The Heads from the rockpools

F rom 1880 to the beginning of WWI the Mosman area and Balmoral in particular became known for its sophisticated, elaborate and permanent "camps". They were mainly occupied by young city workers who liked to enjoy the beach on weekends and in their spare time.

The camps usually had a piano. Some even put together an orchestra of sorts. It is recorded that the "Gipsy Camp" welcomed an Italian Opera Company which was visiting Sydney. The company, dressed in stage costume, performed a show which featured a tenor, called Signor Banchi. Apparently the camp hosts found pronunciation of his name difficult and instead called him "The Sinner".

Other Balmoral camps were "Euroka" and "Artists" (which was established at Edwards Beach and included the company of Streeton, Daplyn, Weston and Livingston Hopkins).

There was also the "Lotus" camp which caused some curiosity because of its grave which was decorated with a seashell mosaic. No one knew who was in the grave. However, when the land was resumed by the Council the decision was made to remove the remains and reinter them. When the ground was dug up the only thing found was a headstone with, " In memory of our beloved dog, 'Umber'!"

Paraphrased from P.R.Stephenson's *Sydney Sails*

Paul Macken

Tony Bartholomew, former Mr Australasia

Backless Costumes Banned at Balmoral

ackless bathing costumes are to be banned at Balmoral Beach.

At Mosman Council on Tuesday night, Ald. Benson said he hoped the Mayor would empower the beach rangers to deal with persons wearing backless bathing costumes. He believed women wearing such costumes had appeared at Balmoral on Sunday.

Ald. Dave Smith said it had been brought under his notice that on Sunday morning two motor car loads of people came to Balmoral Beach, two of the ladies wearing backless bathing costumes. He hoped council would prevent ladies wearing such costumes which were not nice. Ladies should know that council objected to this class of bathing costume.

The Mayor said he would have inquiries made, and anything objectionable in the way of bathing costumes would be banned.

The Daily, Monday 28 October 1929

An American dancer practises her routine one Sunday morning.

OPPOSITE: *The Balmoral Braves, 1996*

Sydney bushfires rage in early 1994 and a strange light envelops the beach.

Friday night triathlon

Shearer's Balmoral Beach Baths, Mosman

HOURS FOR BATHING:

LADIES. – Monday, Wednesday and Saturday,

from 10 a.m. to 1 p.m. Tuesday, Thursday and Friday,

from 2 p.m. to 5 p.m. Holidays excepted.

GENTLEMEN. – At all other hours of the day till 9 p.m.

DUAL BATHING. – One evening in the week.

The Baths may be hired for parties in the evening.

Ladies and Gentlemen taught Swimming.

Refreshments, Hot Water, &c., always on hand.

Friday night triathlon

The *Mosman Mail*, 1 October 1900

Dogs Winning Balmoral Beach 'War'

Dogs which foregather at Balmoral Beach in the early hours of the morning are providing a "headache" for Mosman Council as well as for local residents.

According to a council official, the beach seems to have a fascination for dogs from all over the district. They may even come from other municipalities!

Despite signs warning of dire penalties for anyone who takes a dog on the beach, the dogs find their way to the beach without assistance from their owners — if they have any.

Balmoral Baths

OPPOSITE: *"Patch"*

Some of them are "old timers" who have been going down for a swim and a game for years. They apparently belong to the Icebergs' Club, for they go there all the year round.

They are particularly happy, however, when they can scamper among the early morning swimmers, kicking sand on to those trying to get a healthy tan in the early morning sunshine.

It is not unknown for them to have great games with swimmers' beach towels. Two dogs — one at each end of a towel — can provide delightful entertainment, although it may not be appreciated by the towel's owner!

The problem is, however, what can be done about the dogs?

There is no "open season" for stray dogs — in fact many of the residents (they probably don't live near the beach) appear to be on the dogs' side! And quite a number of aldermen are dog lovers!

Should the council incur the expense of sending a ranger — or rangers — to the beach in the early hours of the morning?

What would be the ratepayers' view of such expenditure?

And, if a ranger were sent, would he be able to catch the dogs?

Some of the dogs are "old hands" at evading capture and would welcome a game of hide and seek! "

The Daily, Thursday 16 March 1961

OPPOSITE: "Spud" and "Olive", Bathers' Pavilion.

Walkies on the bridge

M a d a m   C l u t h a

T he lady who is known by the above cognomen is in no way so mysterious as the name. She is a native of Australia, tall, straight as an arrow, agile, and athletic, with fair hair, and a blonde, candid, earnest face, full of animation. The reason she has this name is because she is a professional, a teacher of swimming. She has been giving lessons to our young people at the Balmoral Baths, that it is hoped will be of benefit to them all their days long.

She is a splendid diver, and has saved several lives. One lady's gratitude shows in keeping her supplied with stationery, and sending her a Christmas box, every year. It is to be hoped she will be properly appreciated by residents and visitors to Mosman, Bondi &c.

The *Mosman Mail*, March 1 1899

Nippers, Balmoral Beach Club

OPPOSITE: Balmoral Baths

Model yacht race

Surf at Balmoral

Band Performance at Balmoral Beach

NEXT SUNDAY EVENING

The popular Northern Suburbs Band will give another performance at the Rotunda, Balmoral Beach, on Sunday evening next, commencing at 8 o'clock.

The last evening performance proved a great success, and attracted large numbers of visitors, who enjoyed good music in ideal surroundings.

Arrangements have been made with the Department of Road Transport and Tramways to provide additional transport facilities for the convenience of those attending the performance.

Amongst the items to be played are a number of popular selections, viz., "H.M.S. Pinafore," "Cavalcade," a march, "The Washington Greys," a waltz medley, "The Gay Nineties," a popular number "Kiss Me Goodnight, Sergeant Major," a march "The Royal Australian Navy" and a cornet solo "The Bostonian". The full programme will be set out in to-morrow's issue of this paper. Deck chairs will be available at a nominal charge of 3d.

The Daily, Friday March 1 1940

OPPOSITE: The Rotunda, 1.30 am

Christmas party at the Watermark

OPPOSITE: *The Watermark*

Queenwood girls at their drawing lesson.

The Esplanade

The construction of the Esplanade and Rotunda was by no means free of controversy. Although the 3 January 1930's *Sydney Morning Herald* referred to the completion of the Esplanade (then called "Lawry Parade") as the '... apple of the council's eye', then Alderman Dave Smith and Mayor Buckle were not re-elected to Mosman Council in 1932. Dave Smith explained his understanding of matters as, "My colleagues in the last two councils have made improvements to the beachfront which to my mind, have made Balmoral Beach the most delightful spot in Sydney; but as the electors think we have been 'concrete mad', they have given Mr Buckle and me the grand order of the boot" (*Mosman Daily* 6 January 1932.)

The Beach Defence Committee fought against the construction of the Rotunda. The Mosman Daily of 7 June 1930 reported a Committee member as stating, "... (if) Council wanted to beautify the beach, let them plant trees".

The Bathers' Pavilion, Balmoral:
A Conservation Plan, Volume 1, July 1994

Juggler

Esther Road

The Bathers' Pavilion

On August 21, 1928 at 3.30 pm Alderman Harry Carter
laid the foundation stone. This was only three months after the
foundation stone of the Bondi Pavilion was laid.
On Wednesday 20th February 1929 the Pavilion was opened
by Mayor Alderman A. Buckle in front of a large gathering of
visitors, parliamentarians and citizens.
The first three year lease of the Pavilion was won
by Mr R.C. Shearer.

OPPOSITE: Bathers' Pavilion window

Edward peering into the Bathers' Pavilion window.

OPPOSITE: *Bathers' Pavilion window*

Fixing the shark net

"In September 1935 the Council accepted a £900 tender
for a steel net enclosure to be suspended from a cable
hung between the end of the Island and a 23-feet-high
tripod opposite the northern end of the Pavilion.
The net was taken down at the end of each summer,
and so avoided most of the kelp blown in to the beach
by easterly gales, usually during winter. Summer and
winter the wire cable was a roost for seagulls, resting there
like pearls on a necklace, and this became another
of Balmoral's charms."

Mosman A History

OPPOSITE: *After the storm*

On Edwards' Beach

"Mosman's Edwardian years were not without tragedy. Just before Christmas Day, 1907, a young man, Henry C. Jones, a member of a "picnic party" was taken by a shark in Middle Harbour on Saturday afternoon, December 21st. He had been swimming with a friend who had left the water to get dressed at the time of the attack. The friend rowed out in a boat to see the victim rise out of the water for the second time and then disappear. On Boxing Day another picnic party found Jones's body at Sugar Loaf Point."

Mosman: Edwardian Years 1901-1911

Baby shark

Dublin Tom

From Art Collector to Cave Dweller

A newspaper wrote of him:

In 1887, Thomas Burgess, Art buyer and Connoisseur of Dublin, arrived in Australia. He brought with him £11,000 of Objets d'Art. To-day at the age of 75 he lives in a sea-shore cave at Balmoral. He is known to his cronies as "Dublin Tom". He says "My father and I had some beautiful stuff when we landed here. We had Sheraton and Chippendale that we bought under the hammer at Christie's. People in Australia didn't appreciate it then. We had to sell it at less than its value". Since then "Dublin Tom" has been miner, labourer, station-hand and farmer.

Tom's final residence was in the cave opposite the Balmoral Baths, wherein for centuries before the blacks had resided.

Perhaps it would best explain many things if the rest of this chapter lapsed into the first person, as "Tom" was a friend of my youth, and I have later discovered that I have absorbed a measure of contentment from that association. For the youth of the Nineties there was little in the way of organised sport, upon which they could work off their abundant energies. We were thrown on our own resources for our own amusement, other than perhaps a game of football, and an occasional sailing race. Naturally, our uncontrolled activities were such as just to keep us one jump from the parental strap — if we were lucky. We were often not lucky. Bird-nesting, the sampling of the fruits of the many orchards, the inspection of the lobster and fish traps of others, and the annoying of innocent Chinese vegetable hawkers, were some of the diversions of the day, and the suburb afforded plenty of room to manoeuvre about — and run when necessary — which was often!

The "characters" were all kind to us, but it is to be regretted that with the ignorance of youth, it was often repaid in the form of playing some practical joke on one of them. One such still lingers, although over the years I feel I have many times repaid its perpetration on "Dublin Tom".

I induced him to enter as a contestant in a Friday Night Vaudeville Trial at the then one and only Picture Show on the site of the present Kinema. It was a very crude affair, open to the sky, narrow wooden benches in the earth for seats. Still, the Entrance Charge was only 3d. and if it rained before half-time, this was refunded. No picture ever went through unless the film broke a few times, whereat the audience would yell derisively until joined together again by an exasperated attendant.

Dublin Tom

The local Fire Brigade had entered a contestant who, by virtue of his age, long beard and the strumming on a violin of one string, had won on no less than three occasions.

We borrowed a full dress suit for Tom, hosed him down and groomed him for his appearance, little worrying what he would do – sing, dance or recite. We considered his immaculate and altered appearance was sufficient in itself to win the popular vote. To our great astonishment, and gratification, Tom rose to the occasion, and in a well-trained baritone, with all his Dublin brogue behind it, demanded "Don't let them sell Killarney". He won the thirty shillings First Prize, and disappeared while we collected our small bets from the Fire Brigade supporters.

This now becomes a story of a dress suit. It had been borrowed, without his knowledge, of course, from Mick Bourke, then licensee of the Buena Vista Hotel, a compatriot and great friend of Tom's. Both were of the same substantial rotund figure.

Mick himself was at the Show, and had great delight in personally sending the singer a bouquet, a well-decorated cabbage, little knowing that the embarrassed Tom was blushing, not at the praise, but at the deception.

Tom was rescued at closing time, and the dress suit, in a shocking state brought about by its wearer's imbibations, was returned to the owner's wardrobe, there to await its next appearance at the Annual Hospital Ball. It never appeared, however. Stained and mildewed, it was permanently bestowed upon Tom.

For years afterwards, housewives answering a knock on the back door at about 6 a.m., would be startled to find a collarless figure, clad in otherwise full evening kit, enquiring "Would you be wanting any fresh fish, lady?" and then stand amazed, as Tom, cleaning the fish, would give it a final wipe on the tails of the suit, and hand it over ..."That'll be 9d. lady, and bless you."

The Mosman That Was 1789-1900, D. (Jack) Carroll, 1949

A flying fox hangs in a Port Jackson fig tree. But where is he?

Lovers on the beach

Father and daughter

Rendezvous on the Island

"BACCHANALIAN ORGIES"
AT BALMORAL BEACH FEARED

A vexed question – whether to provide
facilities for barbecues at the southern end
of Balmoral Beach – was debated at a
meeting of Mosman Council.
One alderman expressed fears during
the discussion that the barbecues could lead
to "Bacchanalian Orgies" !

The Daily, 1964

Lovers on the Island

Dry land sailing, the Esplanade.

Acknowledgements

With special thanks to Sharon Muir, Mosman Library, for her generous assistance.

PAGE 8:
Paraphrased from *Tales of Old Mosman* by Don McLaren.
Published with the permission of the Mosman Historical Society

PAGE 10:
From *Sydney Sails* by P.R. Stephenson, page 50.
Published with the permission of the Royal Sydney Yacht Squadron

PAGE 12:
From *Historical Anecdotes and Miscellany* Article dated 16 July 1930.
Published with the permission of the Mosman Historical Society.

PAGE 14:
The *Mosman Mail*.
September 1, 1899

PAGE 19:
Paraphrased from P.R. Stephenson's *Sydney Sails*, page 71.
Published with the permission of the Royal Sydney Yacht Squadron.

PAGE 20:
The Daily, Monday 28 October 1929.
Published with the permission of the *Mosman Daily*

PAGE 24:
The Daily, Thursday 16 March 1961.
Published with the permission of the *Mosman Daily*

PAGE 34:
The Daily, Friday March 1 1940.
Published with the permission of *The Mosman Daily*

PAGE 36:
From *The Bathers' Pavilion, Balmoral:
A Conservation Plan, Volume 1*
The Report Prepared for Mosman Municipal Council by Robert A. Moore Pty Ltd, July 1994, page 9.
Published with the permission of R.A. Moore. (In acknowledgement of the historical research of Catherine Macarthur).

PAGE 44–45:
From *Mosman A History* by Gavin G. Souter, page 207.
Published with permission of the Melbourne University Press.

PAGE 46:
From *Mosman: Edwardian Years 1901-1911* by Marion McFarlane, page 10.
Published with the permission of Marion McFarlane, MA

PAGE 50:
Excerpt from *The Mosman That Was 1789-1900*, compiled by D. (Jack) Carroll, December 1949, Appendix pages G2, G3 and G4.
Published with the permission of the Mosman Historical Society.

PAGE 53:
The Daily, Saturday, 12 December 1964.
Published with the permission of the *Mosman Daily*.

Here he is

Published by Pt 78 Pty Limited
ACN 003 152 136
PO Box 351
Collaroy Beach NSW 2097
AUSTRALIA
Phone: 61 2 9971 6857
Fax: 61 2 9971 6641

© Copyright Pt78 Pty Limited and Robert and Sarah Billington 1997
First Edition Published July 1997
Reprinted October 1997

ISBN 0 646 31772 5

Printed by Toppan Printing Co. (Australia) Pty Ltd
ACN 001 239 210 in Singapore.

Photography: Robert Billington
Research: Sarah Billington
Design: Kathie Baxter Smith, Design Smiths
Co-ordinating Editor: Peter Eastway
Black and White Printing: Warren Bartetzko
Colour Printing: Nulab Australia

Bathers in the mist, Balmoral Beach, Sydney, Australia.
Photography by Robert Billington. Copyright 1997
Published by Pt 78 Pty Limited, PO Box 351 Collaroy Beach NSW 2097. Ph: 61 2 9971 6857

"Spud and Olive", Balmoral Beach, Sydney, Australia.
Photography by Robert Billington. Copyright 1997
Published by Pt 78 Pty Limited, PO Box 351 Collaroy Beach NSW 2097. Ph: 61 2 9971 6857